NO MORE QUIET ENTRANCES

Poems by Troy Schoultz

Luchador Press
Big Tuna, TX

Copyright © Troy Schoultz, 2019
First Edition1 3 5 7 9 10 8 6 4 2
ISBN: 978-1-950380-75-6
LCCN: 2019955188

Design, edits and layout: El Dopa
Author photo: Amie Brownfield
All rights reserved. No part of this publication may be reproduced or transmitted in any form or by any means, electronic or mechanical, including photocopying, recording or by info retrieval system, without prior written permission from the author.

Acknowledgments:

Most of these poems first appeared in the following publications: *Big Hammer, Chiron Review, Exit 7, Indianapolis Review, Misfit magazine, Stand (U.K.), Slipstream, Nerve Cowboy, Pinyon.*

This collection is dedicated to abandoned factories, roadside memorials, third shift employees, thrift stores, Midwestern autumns and latest last chances.

TABLE OF CONTENTS

Obituary of a Mill Town / 1

Niko's Gyros / 2

Overheard Conversation / 3

In a Laundromat, Super Bowl Sunday Morning / 4

Bicyclists & Lightning at 4:00am / 5

The Goodbye Moon / 6

Mix Tapes / 7

Primavera / 9

Burned Alive and Eaten by Bears / 10

Insomniac Astronomy / 11

Drunks in the Nativity / 12

Foreclosure / 14

Dear Alcohol / 15

The Empty Nesters / 16

Wrong Number from a Woman in California / 18

Asylum Point Park, Oshkosh, WI / 20

Kwik Trip off the Highway, 3:20am / 21

First Date / 22

God Shed His Grace on Thee / 23

Aging / 24

Photographs of Cats Who Passed Over / 25

This is What 1am Sounds Like to a Visitor in Chicago / 27

Gravity / 28

Mercury Years / 29

How to Save the Dying in a 24-Hour Supermarket / 30

Christmases at the Turn of the Century / 31

September Dream Fragments / 33

Memory Fragments While Driving Around With
   the Check Engine Light On / 34

Ghost on an Escalator / 35

Some Silent Movies Never Seen to Grow Old / 37

Regret / 38

Halcyon Years / 39

Five Short Poems About Evel Knevel / 41

The Rockstars of my Youth Are Dead or Dying / 42

Three Scenes from a Wisconsin Winter / 43

With Aftertaste of a Resurrection / 45

9/10/2001 / 47

Safety / 49

Rummage Sale / 50

Talking to a Woman / 51

Shaking Clammy Hands with Lucidity / 53

Utopia Parkway, NYC 1972 / 54

Looking for Crystal / 55

Derangement Parade / 56

Dreams, you know, are what you wake up from.
-Raymond Carver

Obituary of a Mill Town

This is a town of lost dog posters and abandoned cars.
Brick factories watch the dead and dying with cataract windows
Broken out of boredom, machines and breakroom guts
Collecting the grimy residue of neglect and lost stability.
Old men get and stay drunk in taverns before noon,
Dreaming of glasses of rain and new wounds bleeding
They stopped punching clocks, but are far from through
Making their wives cry, for how else can they be sure
That they truly love them.
It's only when lightning fragments the sky
And September rain falls like penance
That we feel both safe and haunted,
Like the slumbering rabbit
Out of the owl's reach.
There is a murmured poetry when the streets start to flood
And the streetlight reflection makes the turn lanes
Impossible to identify. There is the music of light box signs
igniting Against the gray and purple evening. This is why
People talk to headstones
And plead negotiations before they die.
It's so damned hard to leave the familiar repetition
Of this terrifying world behind us.

Niko's Gyro's, Saturday at 10:30pm

The kids are acting dodgy, weird, and familiar
Tonight, slouching in a decades old booth. The fluorescent
Lights highlight the twenty four hour red plastic cup benders.
St. Patrick's Day has been drawn out for a week. Niko's
Has remained a constant as other campus bars and shops
Have risen, fallen, and received facelifts. The décor is all
    hole-in-the-wall
Egg shell colored comfort: the grease-splattered Pepsi sign,
    the video game out of order since 2003.
The smell of lamb meat and fresh pita bread soaks into the ceiling,
But the food satisfies after a day or night
Of watery beer and lousy choices. The boys and girls
Talk loudly, use the word *fuck*
In place of awkward pauses. A silverfish slithers
Across the Formica littered with smeared napkins,
Cucumber sauce, and empty ketchup packets.
A pale boy with crimson hair and gold nose ring
Slams his palm upon the insect as the drunk girls scream.
There are high fives all around as I get my carryout,
Exiting through the foggy glass door, envious
Of their wild laughter, their *fuck you's*
And all the gorgeous mistakes that still lay before them.

Overheard Conversation In A Main St. Coffee Shop, The Day After Memorial Day

Voices pull me over the din
of boring, fashionable jazz where there is
no such thing as just coffee. The rain-washed
window makes stoplight faces easier to look at,
sky drops make heartache codes in ripples
of puddles below. A man in a wheelchair
rolls across the neutral tiled floors, a voice
to make up for his useless legs. He calls the waitress
sweetheart and gets away with it. A regular
approaches him, they launch into
a critical theory of Old Wives tales. I listen,
learning about the enzymes in chicken soup
that cure the common cold, a grandmother's
warning of sleeping under full moons in August,
a grandfather who smoked four packs of smokes
a day since age 12, fried and ate six slices of bacon,
two eggs over easy, and topped it off
with three shots of blackberry brandy
every morning like religion. *He was 91
when he hung up his gloves...*
The rain is predicted to last
the rest of the week. I try to remember
if Memorial Day always falls on a Monday
and why should it matter. Slabs of bacon, frying pan grease,
chain-smoking, and blackberry brandy all sound good
on mornings like these, but I'm hesitant to live to 91.

In a Laundromat, Super Bowl Sunday Morning

The parents have given up hope of finding
their daughter, drugged and offered to the ocean,
the newscaster reports before the update
on the fatalities from a shopping plaza gunman's suicide attack.
The televisions, three in all, are hungry for our eyes. I keep
one eye fastened on the foam and swirl of the triple loader,
    the other
trying to spot an image of Christ in my coffee. I count quarters
as the news gives way to images of shoulder-padded
millionaires held as heroes for their ability
to catch, throw and run, uniforms the shade
of comic book panels. I stare back at my coffee
as the final spin cycle kicks in. Still no Messiah,
just the shape of a rocket ship
from a golden age of wonder and costumed heroes,
not the kind housed in stadiums on Sunday afternoons
but the kind imaged and wished on,
able to deflect bullets, eyes like satellite cameras,
zeroing in on oceans, arriving just in time,
saving young women from drowning.

Bicyclists & Lightning at 4:00am

Early riser, insomniac, third shift disciple,
From my kitchen window, with all lights off, I survey
    the street.
Above, the sky is an electric diorama, all ambitionless grey
    and plum hue
With jagged wires of flame, paparazzi bulbs from all the
    world's corners
Silhouetting phone lines and treetops. Suddenly I see them,
A man and woman of undetermined age, dressed if off to
    a picnic
Or party on a yacht, all white shorts and sweaters, and riding
    a bicycle built for two.
Unrattled by the lightning above, the hollow lack of thunder
    and promise of deluge,
They peddle with a lazy ease and grace as if they just bought
The world's owner's manual. He turns his head to speak.
She tilts back her head back, parted lips laugh with eyes
    closed like a B-film actress.
I watch them as the radio plays a forgotten song
From easier days, early to mid-90's or so,
Lyrics about some Gen-X townie being chased by the cops,
Crashing some old lover's apartment after-hours because
There is simply no place left to go.

The Goodbye Moon

With decades of bar bands behind him
And at least three or four rail-mixers over the line,
He dragged his guitar and amp to the roof.
An unsteady aluminum ladder, his ankle tangled
In extension cords and wavering balance,
He managed to not kill himself. He hit
The first chords knowing his neighbors
Would call the cops, but the moon
Was aching and full,
And lush madness flooded him.
Surrounding house windows
Lit dull yellow one by one,
Random shouts, distant sirens rising.
It wasn't goddess worship,
He never considered the moon his lover.
Recalling his stint in film school, he saw it as
A destination, a fugitive oasis with caves
And starlight nightscapes housing
Mêlée's sailor women and exploding men.
Through split lips and broken teeth
He sang cover songs,
Each one about the moon,
Bypassing original composition
Because the only songs he was able to write
    were the kind that
Say goodbye.

Mix Tapes

She misses the age of Aqua Net, White Rain mousse,
pastels, and Molly Ringwald's box office royalty.
Child-free with two divorces in her rearview mirror,
she drives her Toyota Corolla to the city's edge, tears up
backroads, navigates blind across farm country
on weekend nights and vacation days. The only destination
is to get lost. She's made friends with ease, even been asked
  out a few times,
but her need for solo road-trips, the perfume of oncoming
  storms,
and the snare of gravel's percussion under the fenders
are things the girls at the office could never understand.
She keeps a travel mug full of Boone's Farm and ice
and a fresh pack of menthols cigs at the ready. In a box
that once contained photos, she pulls out one of many mix
  tapes
recorded 20 or more years ago, no worse for wear.
She pops it into a relic tape deck slouched
on the passenger seat and presses play.
B-52's *Rock Lobster*, The Cure's *Close To Me*,
early U2, Soft Cell's *Tainted Love*; New Wave
classics spilling from torn speakers
mingle with the early spring air from the open windows.
She, a time traveler, drives her dad's battered
stick shift Ford F-150, roaring towards the lake

to meet her scholarship boy with the nightfall eyes.
He'd slide his hands under the elastic of her cotton panties,
push the limits of her heart and live forever,
slightly vampiric, in Instamatic photos.
Lightning's wire splits the horizon. She presses
the pedal with a pedicured, sandaled foot,
still in that battered pick-up,
chasing twilight into two decades removed,
the blurred rows of corn, her voice orchestral,
sweetened with discount wine and Newport lights
singing word for word
every lyric to Pretty in Pink.

Primavera

I can't explain my sullen nature
or its shadowy arrivals. I drink whiskey sours
in this Italian restaurant and storm clouds descend.
You speak of marriages, I know your needs.
People change, all wear masks sideways.
I say as much draping our table in silence.
I reach for bread and olive oil, desperate
for truce. The conversation around us
unnerves me. Winter drifts through
our table window, I would risk
our lives together for an escape clause.

My plate of gnocchi arrives in white sauce
and peas. I confused primavera for a red sauce.
Accept it or send it back? A drunken father,
toothless, relief map face, slurs as his
children laugh at him. Will this dish be wasted
if returned? Murals and faux statues
glare, burning through me. Capacity seating eyes
seem in wait or judgment.
You may love me all you wish,
I will one day disappoint you.

Burned Alive and Eaten by Bears

If you ever did hard time for writing bounced checks
And had your head busted open behind bars
Over a poker game misunderstanding
You might develop a stutter and have a tough time
Corralling the thoughts that swim like piranhas
In the back of your eyes. You also might find yourself
Living in a Dutch windmill themed motel
Complete with a miniature windmill missing a propeller or two
And in desperate need of a paint job.
You'd while away the hours missing your children
And the wife who left you. You'd devise little mental lists
Such as the worst possible ways to die. Being dead
Is child's play, it's the dying that's hard. Being shredded
By the claws of a grizzly would be bad, but being burned alive is
Less than favorable. This is how you'd possibly while away time
As you eat packaged hot dogs and ramen noodles, amazed
    and despondent
At how you came to this place, taking a shower four times a day
Out of boredom and watching the sunset paint your eggshell
Walls like cheap aquarium coral.

Insomniac Astronomy

We search out the dim flicker of Venus
When it is much too late. Seek out constellations
Of suns long dead tearing through science
Hanging like grains of glass above us.
We are exhausted, and have driven heavy miles.
We fall into bed and I listen to the sound
Of you falling like stars left uncounted.
I adjust my weight besides you,
Pray against any 3 a.m. lost souls
Who don't hold our best interests at heart.

My eyes close as shadows scrawl a sick doubt,
Because shadows cannot touch love.
Love is full currency, it transforms
But never loses value, and when someone
Loves you, you best take notice,
Never ignore it, treat it like an earthquake
That needs to replace and rearrange,
Fold us against the regulation
Of all that ignites and cools
The suns we attempt to identify
When our eyes are burning
And the sky contains
Each and every color at once.

Drunks in the Nativity

They snuck in at the Christmas light show and fund raiser,
Bypassing usual traffic, perishable good donation check
    points, wandering
Blatant, fearless rejects, wild, blind piloted in automatic.
Barging in, sending statues of Joseph and Mary aside,
    manhandling
The infant Christ. No gold, frankincense or myrrh, just
    rotgut supermarket brand vodka
And generic lemon/lime soda in Solo cups. Neon Stars of
    Bethlehem flashed above
Along with the movement of confectionary electric color
    spanning the park,
Bare branches and evergreens both. Gingerbread villages
    pulsed as Andy Williams
Sang through the decades about what he claimed to be the
    most wonderful time of the year,
Never mind the scary ghost stories and tales of past glories
whatever the hell those might be.
The families passing through look away, even the actors
    playing Mr. and Mrs. Clause
Stroll by, too embarrassed to witness. Security is busy
    collecting
Unperishable and monetary donations. The inebriated
    manger occupants launch into

"Oh Holy Night", caterwauling with painful sincerity.
The audience hesitates, teased by something brushing up
    close to
A tarnished display of the sacred.

Foreclosure

He reads the raindrops
like some suspicious code,
doesn't answer his ringtone, wishes
phones didn't exist. Outside
leaves bleed and fall, clogging
street drains, blanketing lawns.
The mailbox spills postmarked threats,
He closes the blinds, breaks another seal,
pours another day on ice.

Dear Alcohol

You draped me in crimson capes
and kicked me off skyscrapers,
slapped six guns to my shins, left me stranded
surrounded by gunfighters in Deadwood,
rolled me like a two-tongued whore with a PhD,
made some vacant nights nuclear,
my forearms, raw with paper-cuts
from ace cards in hiding.

I miss your amber kingdoms,
holding court with an anvil tongue.
Glassfuls of hot-wired vocabulary,
rented persona, stuntman-for-hire.
I back-slapped bikers with inked biceps
praising your name, flirted raw with their half-naked,
midnight-haired women, somehow
managed to linger among
after-hours sidewalks and streetlights,
still breathing, in one piece, alive.

You've left me a porcelain head haloed with echo,
throbbing, dark as licorice, my name as lightning
etched on brushed aluminum, frosted glass,
all my tiny loves reduced to chalk lines and urban legends,
or seagulls and dumpster mornings,
five in the morning skylines hemorrhaging color.

The Empty Nesters

Your starter home took root,
became the satellite of neighborhood activities,
a quarter century of marriage celebrated, the garages glow
    like cathedrals,
the grill is cooking, the beer on ice, you feel almost guilty
to be celebrating a quarter century of marriage with the
    impending
divorce happening three doors down the block. The backyard
    fires embers
whisper, the downtown taverns begin to clear. You drift off
    to sleep
under the influence of a neighbor's seventy-year-old brandy.

You sleep next to your wife in a house
with vacated rooms. No more quiet entrances after midnight,
no weekend headlight approaching or backing out
nor refrigerator raids, there is little left
to stay awake for.

Early Sunday a.m., you back your pickup from the driveway.
These are the mornings you wish the communion wine
Would ease away last night's liquor. You spot your youngest
    son's truck
Parked outside the home of the 36 year-old divorcee down
    the block.

You wish him luck with all his future mistakes, and let it go.
Your memory drifts to college diplomas, cheap, leaking
   plumbing rentals,
delivering pizzas for side cash, a July marriage,
a down payment on a starter home.

Wrong Number From a Woman in California Who is Concerned About Global Warming

She asks if I've been done in with republican brain-
 washing.
I answer no, I haven't been done in with democratic
 brain-washing either.
She tells me she lives in Berkley, and has read of the
 evidence
Of ice cap melting. It both fascinates and frightens her.
She asks if the young girls in Wisconsin abuse the word *like*
In loose conversation and affect a nasally accent.
I tell her that we of the central north
Have dialect issues all our own. She says she is originally
From Buffalo but there is nobody left there for her.
She speaks of a nasty divorce, says her ex-husband stole
 her journals.
What a bastard, I say. She tells me it was fair,
That she swiped his book of hieroglyphics.
You are both thieves and deviants, I tell her. She laughs
 and mentions
That she is an artist, which would explain her talking to a
 wrong number
For well over ten minutes. I tell her this
And she laughs like rain. I don't know if I'm delighted
Or saddened to realize that this is the highlight
Of my brandy-soaked Friday evening.

Her musical voice trails off until she offers me her name
- Susan -
And she wishes me a good night. The line goes dead.
It's the 5th of December, forty-five degrees outside and raining

Asylum Point Park, Oshkosh, WI

It never held signaled navigational light, never beckoned
Boats to shore or direction on Lake Winnebago.
Canadian geese, indifferent to us leave gifts of feathers
Scattered below, enough to build
An Icarus starter kit. Moonlight and misplaced lightning
lived In the heads of those from the asylum, who were allowed
Time in the sun to construct this lighthouse. Many are buried
On these grounds, stones engraved with numbers not names.
No exorcism, fishing, or picnics can erase the loneliness here.

After the sun falls, the moon leaks on the lake's reflection,
And mother owls hunt for their young.
The rugged stone tower leads to a milky glass womb.
In the dark they appear with the deer and rabbits
In the clearing, the builders rise and walk,
Admiring their craftwork, making their way
In the summer haze with the singular grace that ordinary
Ghosts can somehow never pull off.

Kwik Trip off the Highway, 3:20 am

Red taillights flicker, settle and die from the distance
Complementing the blazing lightbox sign.
There's comfort among coolers, aisles, and coffee machines,
Soups and chowders, pizza by the slice,
Corndogs two for two dollars.
The sleepless drive here in cars
Stinking of burnt oil and impossible debt.
The waxed floors reflect overhead light
Dim enough to sooth bloodshot eyes
As native bones far below the foundation
Lying restless and cheated tremble, dance, and grow halos.
Shift workers, runaways, and insomniacs
Choose their caffeine of choice and ingredients of loneliness.
Truckers pull their rigs
With interiors wallpapered in snapshots and porn
From out of the parking lot as frogs and crickets
Sing and legends of upright wolves
Walk the woods of Wisconsin, and scatter as
An orange tinge steals witchcraft from the pines.
The highway blooms with traffic
Crawling back to the empty arms and low snores
And all the reasons they continue to work under false sunlight
And sleep away the hours of the day.

First Date

Outside the sun has dropped through asphalt.
Gut level honesty
Becomes the liability. We talk
After midnight. Thinking, pausing,
Tossing back brandy. Lust is a gargoyle
Riding the shoulders of angels, a gun barrel
Against the forehead of comfort.
Try this night on for size
And switch off your lights, we could
Fall down the stairs of this life holding
On to each other.
She told me to walk west
Until I can't remember my hands on her skin...
And I like the moon when it hangs like a shard of porcelain...
And yes, I love the sound of forgotten guitars...
Why must I keep up the talking? I can't be the one to entertain you.
I'm not getting paid a union salary for this. Speak and tell,
Stop fingering that glass of wine and bail me out of this.
It's too soon since I lost her.
You can't expect my charm to last.
A coin-toss neighborhood, an hourglass of hearts thirsting
The world's great curtains of sleep.
My latest last chance.

God Shed His Grace on Thee

A younger woman with too much make-up,
Sweatpants and bird nest hair
Shrieks at her child because he was born,
Pleads to have another check cashed
Before the month's end. Two girls
Man the counter of the Check 2 Ca$h Quick Loan,
College fresh, tanned, unscarred,
Watch this alien's performance.
They explain to her the interest percentage,
Refuse her check, their robotic patience
And sympathy dimming with the late-afternoon
Sun. A man looks around the room
Trying to meet downcast eyes,
Looking for some dignity on overdraft faces.
The perfume of fresh carpet and new furniture
Mixes with the stink of lost jobs and debt.
His stomach feels like a fist,
His fists wanting to connect
With skin, teeth and bone.
Outside battered, dying cars gather
Thirsty for a lie of a new beginning,
Hoping for the mirage of temporary mercies.

Aging

There is something dark and unrelenting
about seconds becoming hours
and hours turned to years.
Don't let them tell you
those candles are just numbers,
they are the black eyed children
you invite into your home after 2AM. Numbers can turn on you
like a campfire neglected. People you love will fade in the smoke.
Ghosts are the currency of the young. In age they become
    composites,
following you through displaced calendars,
passing before you in bathroom mirrors
before the teaser light of dawn.

Photographs of Cats Who Passed Over

Scamp, 2001
A furry gray bluesman
with a great plumage tail,
singing and moaning outside my window.
Some nights he'd be out later than I was
comfortable with. I'd pull up a lawn chair
to the make-shift backyard fire pit.
I'd sip German beer darker than the sky,
waiting for his entrance from the shrubs. I'd pretend
to not see him, pouncing into my lap, tucking in his front legs
as I scanned the stars for UFOs,
soaking in the quiet until
the night's edge turned a whisper of orange.

Violet, 1975
1974 shows me holding you
On my Grandmother's front lawn,
deep yellows and orange tint of Kodak snapshots.
When we found out you were male
it was too late to change your name.
There's the one picture of you
crawling from out of my father's boot.
You were a genius of escape,
no locks or screens could hold you.
Taffy, 1996

A tortoise shell, talkative,
copper pennies eyes
An ex-girlfriend surrender you to me.
She moved out, you stayed, and my life was
soon to implode, I gave you up to another.
You never recovered.
You over groomed until empty patches of skin appeared.
You were an elegant old woman
In a tattered fur coat who died broken hearted.

This Is What 1am Sounds Like
To a Visitor in Chicago

It's not the low whine of police and ambulance sirens.
We have those in Oshkosh. It's the blunt hum of the a/c
Shuddering and wheezing like a black lung victim. It's the drip-
Drip of sweat upon me. It's the lack of dollars and direction,
Concrete, glass and steel spiraling to clouds
Where the hell are the trees, squirrels and lakes?
It's falling to sleep in a city without eye contact
And waking to the rage of traffic.
Feel the night,
Respect its rusted offerings.

Gravity

Pull a chain
And autumn leaves will rain upon you
In a tomb of snow

Close your eyes, one at a time
And you are closer to me
Than blood or memory

Call for me
If the sound of your voice
Will dissolve clocks and calendars

Fall upon me
When you no longer care enough to cry
And the clouds seem poised
To fall upon you

Mercury Years

Too easy at age twenty-five to thirty to laugh off
the crows against grey Sunday skies, obituaries,
white pills to keep our hearts
from turning on us, the bone on bone
of a knee screaming for mercy.
These things now bring me to dull silence,
march me to that place where
it was easy to run across the grass and sand,
drink this, swallow that, and fake immortality
in borrowed cars.

This is the year we went
From the funereal white of winter
into summer's furnace breath.
Leaves and gardens heavy with sun and rain,
makes us forget the frozen months
like an alcoholic forgets his last drunk gone bad.
The years spill and run like mercury,
be it a wing helmeted Roman god
or toxic beads from a shattered thermometer.
These are the days of porch lights lit for loss
and a waiting closet of gift-wrapped goodbyes,
leaving us hungry for early rain to melt snow,
for autumn to burn hard against winter's crawl.

How to Save the Dying In a 24 Hour Supermarket

Faces white-washed under florescent lighting,
cloistered of closed registers,
of all the forgotten songs, *Love Will Tear Us Apart*
spills from the overhead speakers like an after-thought.

A single mother, second shift refugee, a cart
of juice drink boxes and lunch meat, draws his eyes,
full and panicked as bloody summer moons,
summoning the light of a heaven,
or Christ, or a patron saint of lost causes,
her chapped lips mouth the words
It will all be okay. Go home. Sleep.
His hands pull away the bottles, allowing
the laundry and dish soaps to pass, the oranges
colliding like dancing suns across the black conveyer.

Christmases at the Turn of the Century

(1999)
My ex and I strung the lights on the tree,
Drank tequila and listened to Queen's Greatest Hits.
I cannot tell you if it was forty degrees or forty below.
Previous summer she kicked me out. I moved
In with a junkie/alcoholic friend who wrote poems
And made portraits of Jesus out of colored tiles.
His place was all chipped paint and bad plumbing.
She invited me back at the dog park.
Said she missed me.
By the following summer I moved into
A chipped painted structure with bad plumbing
All of it's own.

(2001)
Noon hours, downtown Oshkosh, all gray skies
And slushy sidewalks. I met this Earth Mama .
We'd attend organ recitals each Wednesday
At whatever churches housed pipe organs.
She gave me an E. Powers Biggs CD.
I gave her my indecision. Previous August she
Gave me homegrown tomatoes. December,
I gave her the one line that makes even
The kindest and best of women disappear;
Let's try to stay friends.

(2002)
I stared into the blizzard and thought
About dying. Nothing suicidal, just
What it would feel like to disappear
like an owl among barn rafters.
Brandy was like water or milk to me.
Bubbling lights lined
The window sills held with Scotch tape.
I was turning grey already,
Over the threshold of thirty,
Trying to convince myself
That I didn't fuck up beyond repair.
And no,
If you are willing to ask,

I didn't bother with a goddamn tree, had no
New Year's resolutions to speak of.

September Dream Fragments

A buck danced on my front lawn
In the flicker of an early sun,
Hooves leaving prints of the frosted, dying grass.
It was primal, pagan, a song of forgotten gods.

There are owlets nesting in a dying tree.
The wooden owl statue from Mexico
Comes to life and clings to me.
A tiny parakeet rests on my finger.
A newborn bay reaches out and crushes it.

An overcast day, driving through various states.
I'm in my early twenties, and it's the 1990's.
Rain on my windshield. I come to an old movie theater.
The lobby is ornate with golden curtains.
A lot of cowboy types in the audience.
On the screen, an old farmer with shaking hands
Drinks a glass of wine as red as blood.
It spills down the front of him
And stains the screen.
I wake up and I am old again.

Memory Fragments While Driving Around With the *Check Engine* Light On

I woke up to the sound of collision outside my window,
And stayed awake, thirsting the dim energy of 4am
To make me feel something again. Flashing red and blue
    lights flooded the room,
Your voice looks like it's rushing past.

I often dream of being young and unaware of dying. I awaken
To aching knees, sore hands and a lousy sense of balance.
Lisa, with your love of predatory cats and saxophone,
Is time still on our side?

A teacher and writer once told me
When I was young and drunk
To write short stories and expect
A life of bad love.

She asked if she could stay in my office
While I graded papers.
Her eyes were Christmas and Halloween combined.
She could've been my life's mistake.

Ghost on an Escalator

Her lips could make your ears ring,
her nylon thighs could birth lightning
She would have the gift of grace
in stiletto heels or cowboy boots, exiting off the escalator
through the glass doors and into memory, her dress flows
a flag of all that is holy of summer. A city of millions,
no eye contact, widening distances, yet we latch on
to the random one, imaging them falling
like certain leaf and projecting into your life
fireworks ribbons against a cloudless night.
The tragedy of aging is that you start to fade
in the eyes of these breathing artworks,
startling as any sculpture, more powerful than a poem.
The snow gathering in your hair, you find yourself
a ghost riding this elevator. A song from the 1980's
is resurrected from the overhead sound system
and you are transported back to an empty park
And the first girl who let you kiss under a heavy witchcraft
    moon,
your hand awkwardly sliding down the front of her cutoff
    shorts,
Forever cursed by the found miracle,
her quickened breath, her cherry flavored tongue
entwined yours until her father found you both,
the horn blaring from his battered van.

You start to wonder if your thoughts are legal
as you step off the same escalator, through the same glass doors
and the ghost in you only imagined her walking into the sun,
because the clouds are hanging low and moody
but the rain suddenly tastes like sugar.

Some Silent Movies Never Seem to Grow Old

I've always related to classic movie monsters.
Take for instance Lon Chaney's 1925 portrayal of the Phantom.
Now mad Erik was no saint, I'll grant you that—
causing chandelier vandalism, strangling stage hands,
acting rough around the edges with the beautiful Christine.
It's what you become after years of stagnant water, no sunlight,
a coffin for a bed and a face like a skull. But he was a romantic,
    damn it all,
and love, true love, can make a lunatic out of the best of us.
No, it's the crazed, united torch and pitchfork militias
that always repulsed me, stupid in fury,
righteous in vigilante, cowards drunk
on vigilante gut-rot.
These are the true horrors of this poem.

Regret

Regret dances about you like Hell's own jagged-limbed shadows
After 1 am when you are alone and sleep ignores
Your spend-the-night come-ons, leaving you
Lusting oblivion all the more.

A poet friend once told me that writers are
Selfish bastards, selfish with their time, selfish with their feelings,
Selfish with love. He lives in the country,
Drinks strong coffee, lifts weights, watches horror movies
From the 1980's and embraces solitude like the lovers
We can't afford to keep.

I want to be the piano key toothed man being interviewed
Who claims regrets don't exist on his personal plane.
I at least want to be Sinatra with regrets *too few to mention.*

Regret is a ghost captured on video in your backyard after
    sundown.
It creeps in your head like camera flash residue, the messages
    so deadly honest
You wished them back as soon as they were sent, the absence
    of my heart
When some need it most, words like knives
Stabbing across the years.

Halcyon Years

Everybody knows who died when,
What tavern stood where,
and who the bartenders were.
Everybody who was born here,
became an adult and never left
knows secrets, who was sleeping
with who, who's lover
burnt down whose house
with incense and scented candles.

Too many secondhand latest last chances,
too many venom debts and pig iron anchors,
too many brain cells dim from
desperate last call weekends,
the antique store's basement filled
with yellowing wedding albums and yearbooks
scrawled in masturbating hands
with declarations of unending parties
and clumsy gropes at romance.

Through the curtain humidity
of mid-summer nights,
Ghosts of drive-in movie screens rise
from clay soil fields and cataract windows
of abandoned factories burn warm
and birth hues like cathedrals.

With a lunch box in the refrigerator
And the coffee-maker on timer, a man sleeps gifted
With teenage cornucopia dreams
of that one redhead he met twenty-five years ago
at the Quick Mart looking bored as a Tuesday
with cherry Chapstick lips
and a sugar-razored tongue,
beaches under pale moons,
Green-lit dashboards
and reckless oaths of escape.

Five Short Poems About Evel Knievel

I.
His motorcycle danced behind him
like unforgiving sins,
and fell upon him
like a psychopathic lover.

II.
His rocket-cycle never cleared the divide,
so the snake opened its unhinged jaws to greet him.

III.
Bones broken and welded back,
disciples of self-annihilation and gravity's pain
offer you tribute.

IV.
Hired thugs and aluminum bats
were the tools of your literary critique.

V.
You were good/bad, not evel,
merely a son of a bitch spliced with the DNA
of a cat. Your star-spangled outfit and cycle exhaust
made America forget the smell of napalm
and burning draft cards.

The Rockstars of my Youth are Dead or Dying

I trust my dogs over my cats
Because they have eyebrows
And I can tell what they're thinking.
My right knee howls on overcast mornings
When the rain is making a half-assed effort to fall.
Tomatoes in the garden are ripe and bursting in September,
But I give them away because my damaged kidneys
Can't take the potassium. I stare
At the clothesline posts and consider that rust is slow
 moving fire.
There's not a lot that seems real this autumn. The leaves
Ignite, but the mercury still reaches the seventies.
I don't know what middle ae is supposed to feel like.
My dog with eyebrows knitted in pity considers me a fool.
I still got friends who call on occasion.
They make me laugh when all I want to do
Is drive around with the *Check engine* light on
Like I did when I was twenty, when all was ablaze
Like backyard trees and elevated rust,
And the vinyl record albums I've collected
Like the hours of a decade
Never became obsolete.

Three Scenes from a Wisconsin Winter

I
What sort of a curse could fall upon someone
to make them park their camper in the Marshfield County
    fairgrounds
throughout the month of January when the wind bends
    window panes,
and drifts rise and dance like ghost cotillions?
It must've been biblical.

II
The funereal home across Highway 13 is lit like an upper-class
    motel.
A suicide, plastic bag and suffocation. Not the ideal way to exit,
but effective if you're seeped in desperation. I wonder
if he was too drawn up in this season of endurance,
where the sky and ground are often the same color
and even blue-sky days of sun are cold enough to kill.

III
I'm talking to a trucker at my second job. He's a southerner
and believes we live in God's country, but concedes
that he doesn't understand why every kind of store
sells hard liquor, or the point of ice fishing. But there is faith
in driving 4x4 trucks across Lake Winnebago
where shanty villages grow. Men of patience escaping their
    marriages

sit inside drinking beer and brandy
dreaming idly of next summer's cucumbers and tomatoes,
while sturgeon hover weightless below, gazing through
    ancient eyes.

With Aftertaste of a Resurrection

Streamers rocket overhead, bounce off mirrored walls,
Land at her feet. She hides the scars under
That turtleneck sweater, pulls her silver hair into a bun,
Runs her hand-painted nails around the rim of her chocolate
   martini
And watches the over-the-hill '80's glam band on TV
Trying for a comeback during the latest annual pull towards
   the apocalypse
There is enough darkness and smoke here for camouflage,
   enough dim light
To know these faces as human. When the strangers suck face
   at midnight
She watches them like meerkats on the Discovery channel
And smiles despite being elbow to elbow with kissing strangers.
The confetti spills from the ceiling over her oasis
The dance floor band rushes through
The classic rock songbook for the thousandth time.

She remembers the snowfall
Half a decade or so ago tonight.
Through where the windshield should have been
How the ambulance ripped
A tear into the backdrop of night.
A car full, she flew
Like a new-born angel

From the forehead of God
The only one to never wear her
Seatbelts. Still, she, the only survivor
Who walks and now mouths
Every word to those classic rock songs
Better than the dance floor band or the
New Years host slurring like the devil ripped out his tongue.
This is the stabbing loneliness of the reborn
This is the profane magic
And guilt of Vegas odds survival
The lingering aftertaste of a resurrection.

9/10/2001

Found the receipt,
a poor man's bookmark
between pages of one of several
books I chose to donate
during one of
far too many
moves.

An auto parts store receipt, from a city
I once adopted as my hometown.
Items purchased: air pressure gauge,
STP gas treatment,
windshield washer fluid, two
Slim Jims. Date:
September 10, 2001, 5:42 p.m.
I trace memory back to standing
in the checkout,
the faces next in line.
I imagine
it was sunny out.
I imagine that none of us in line
sensed our lives were on the verge.

We would seep
through automatic doors,
attend to our cars, eat dinner,

watch some T.V., fall asleep
alone or preferably entangled
in the limbs
of someone we loved,
awakening to a morning
that would cure us
of a dream or two.

Safety

He was built like a linebacker or bouncer,
Layered in flannel and denim in August,
Gray hair sprouting from underneath
A robin egg blue hardhat.
Tirelessly he roamed the streets of
Oshkosh, Wisconsin. I figured he was
A construction worker, until it occurred
To me that construction workers
Rarely carry guitar cases.

In another life he was an engineer,
But opted out of
Our frantic daily races
And contests.
Said he was mugged once
In Chicago.

Got hit over the head
With a hammer.
Would be damned
To ever let that
Happen again.

Rummage Sale

He'd been dry for the year
they lived together, because
he loved her and her daughter
and he'd rather take a bullet
than expose either one to madness,
but the landlord and landlady wanted their house back,
and he suddenly relied less and less upon her touch.

An old familiar thirst crept back in his throat.
Both agreed that separate living was the answer
and a rummage sale was in order.
Folding tables and a second-hand stereo transformed
the garage into a thrift boutique
of the collected debris of living.
When she left for work in the morning,
he'd steal one of her clove cigarettes
and mill about the tables filled with mismatched sets
of dishes, novelty kitchen utensils, and clutter.
At night they would lie together in silence. Some nights
She would still roll over and wrap her arm around him.
He would feel her heart beat, breathing,
and another mistake blossoming.
More of their lives disappeared at the end of each weekend
until all that was left was battered and scarred debris
in tote bins and black bags left roadside
in a rearview mirror silhouetted
in a blood orange sunset.

Talking to a Woman Who Feels
Musical Vibrations, Uninhibited Joy
and the Right to Suicide

I spent part of morning
In a superstore parking lot, not wanting to go inside.
I needed hand soap, dental floss, fluoride rinse
And body wash. I sat in my dying Chevy
Watching December rain behind a cracked windshield
Listening to Garrison Keillor on National Public radio
Reading a Kenneth Rexroth poem
About skiing at 3am in subzero temperatures.

I spent the later part of the morning back in bed.
I got only about 2 hours of sleep that night.
I heard noises I cannot account for. I'm making
Serious life changes. I talk to God when I can,
But it is the devil who answers after two a.m.
He calls me a motherfucker in a monotone voice that sounds
As if it traveled beyond decades and frequencies.

I went to a seasonal job late that afternoon,
Jockeying phones, turning down credit to inner city
Dwellers and social security recipients
Wanting to send real Wisconsin cheese to people they loved.
I strike up conversation with the woman
In the cubical next to mine. She is a musician
From Dallas, aged 50 and more driftless than I.

She couldn't decided between moving to
Marshfield, WI and NYC. Like me, she settled on family.
We spoke of the mathematics of music, how sound
Can supplement you like vitamins, how I am not odd in feeling
A weird ecstasy in watching dust mites floating in sunrays
And the smell of wood smoke in November,
And the idea that sometimes when you can't give enough
To an indifferent world you ought to be able
To turn off the neon, set up a closed sign and take a walk.
We both agree on Vincent Van Gogh's suicidal right,
but choose to hang around. There are so many
chords and vibrations, a gourmet buffet
Of loved ones expressions, so goddamn many stars
And sunflowers that have yet to fall upon us.

Shaking Clammy Hands With Lucidity

Half past the three A.M. hour,
A bathroom mirror stare down,
Broken fresh from the ice
Of a nightmare forgotten
Before your eyes sparked
And your breath crossed over,

Your prodded heart
Clashes against a bone jail,
An angry drunk incarcerated.

Through blinds,
All is icy, both spirit and climate.
This sick moon, a porcelain shard
Dangling from a rusted wire.
A starving owl recites her own obituary.

The dead silent film star was right.
There is nothing at all funny
About clowns in the moonlight.

Utopia Parkway, NYC 1972
At the time of his death, the artist Joseph Cornell thinks of the ballerina Tamara Toumanova

Collector of dreamscapes and bubble pipes,
Unmarried, living with mother and invalid brother,
breaking from the collected debris of daydreams,
Climbing the stairs to elevated trains and the ballet.

This one ballerina, dancing Black Swan,
Cyclone of midnight.
Heartbreak, bravos, and rose petal rain.
His world, a basement bench, scattered found fragments,
And discarded mementos.

He immortalized her in a shadowbox,
Sapphire-colored glass,
Cut-outs of suns and castles, snowy feathers.
Letters were exchanged,
They met once or twice.
He waits backstage
Scissors in hand to snip
White feathers from her costume.

Looking for Crystal

Rent's overdue and the grass has overgrown
Tires sizzle against the slick black
wet pavement. There is a lack of parades today
and we're eating my tongue to stop the lies
from spreading. It's a rummage sale kingdom
and the homeless veteran camps outside Pick'n'Save
with frozen pizza cardboard signs *Will Work for Food*.
I'm strung out from a lack of sun and second guesses.
This duplex apartment used to be a grocery store
and the girl with popsicle colored hair turns circles on her
bicycle as sand colored military trucks tool off the factory lot,
Testing their stealth down main street. The flyer ripped and
stapled to the telephone pole says *Looking for Crystal*
and a three-legged black cat shoots a look of hate
and gallops into the shrubs. I miss arcades and
tuna salad sandwiches when it rains two days before June
and the temps barely scrape sixty degrees.
I'm hungry for something that's missing
and we're all just looking for Crystal but
we settle broken glass to sleep upon
and we can't take back the clamor of bells already rung.

Derangement Parade

Marching sideways in a single-file heap
Under a cranberry sun
And xylophone spinal clouds
Pickled-heart jukeboxes play
The closing time seashells,
The falsetto
Oleanders flash
Sunflower eyes,
Lemon sounds of biography arks
And the Dictaphone fists march by.
The inky shot glasses of blank address
A salt wash of arcade devils weaving
A kindergarten sweater.
The surgical
Music of aluminum foil
And ambush chain mail kisses
And my god look at the bearded sky!

They couldn't have picked
A more perfect day.

Troy Schoultz is a lifelong Wisconsin resident. His poems, stories, and reviews have appeared in *Seattle Review, Rattle, Slipstream, Chiron Review, Midwestern Gothic* and several others. He's the author of two chapbooks and one full-length collection: *A Field of Bonfires Sings* (Wolf Angel Press, 1999), *Good Friday* (Tamafyr Mountain Poetry 2005) and *Biographies of Runaway Dogs* (Vegetarian Alcoholic Press, 2017). He teaches for the University of Wisconsin at the Oshkosh and Fox Cities campuses. His interests and influences include rock and roll, playing the bass, found objects, the paranormal, abandoned places, folklore, old cemeteries and the number five.

www.ingramcontent.com/pod-product-compliance
Lightning Source LLC
Chambersburg PA
CBHW030132100526
44591CB00009B/622